I can write
a book
series

I can write a book about
My life

Bobbie Kalman
Crabtree Publishing Company
www.crabtreebooks.com

Created by Bobbie Kalman

Für meine "Schwester" Elfi,
Ich werde immer dankbar sein. Ich liebe Dich.

**Author and
Editor-in-Chief**
Bobbie Kalman

Editors
Kathy Middleton
Crystal Sikkens

Photo research
Bobbie Kalman

Design
Bobbie Kalman
Katherine Berti
Samantha Crabtree
  (logo and cover)

Prepress technician
Katherine Berti

Print and production coordinator
Katherine Berti

Illustrations
Barbara Bedell: p. 9 (bottom left),
  10 (bottom right), 16 (bottom),
  17, 18 (bottom)

Photographs
Istockphoto: p. 14 (top)
Bobbie Kalman: back cover inset,
  p. 5 (top inset), 16 (top left),
  18 (top), 19 (top, center, and
  bottom right inset), 27 (top inset),
  31 (bottom left)
American Red Cross: Dennis Drenner:
  p. 15 (top right)
Shutterstock: cover, logo, title page,
  p. 3, 4, 5 (top book background

and bottom right), 8 (bottom
center and bottom right), 9
(all except center right and
bottom right), 12, 13, 14 (bottom),
15 (top left and bottom), 16 (top
right), 20 , 21 (all except center
right), 22–24, 25 (all except bottom
left), 26, 27 (all except top inset),
28, 29, 30, 31 (top and center);
amskad: p. 9 (bottom right);
Sam DCruz: p. 9 (center right);
Doug James: p. 25 (bottom left);
Jim Parkin: p. 24 (top); Paul
Prescott: p. 21 (center right)
Thinkstock: Photos.com: p. 8 (top left)
Wikimedia Commons: p. 28
  computer inset (*The Old Plantation*,
  commons.wikimedia.org/wiki/
  File: SlaveDance and_Music)

Library and Archives Canada Cataloguing in Publication

Kalman, Bobbie
    I can write a book about my life / Bobbie Kalman.

(I can write a book series)
Includes index.
Issued also in electronic format.
ISBN 978-0-7787-7993-3 (bound).--ISBN 978-0-7787-8002-1 (pbk.)

    1. Autobiography--Authorship--Juvenile literature. 2. Biography
as a literary form--Juvenile literature. 3. Composition (Language
arts)--Juvenile literature. 4. English language--Composition and
exercises--Juvenile literature. 5. Book design--Juvenile literature.
I. Title. II. Series: Kalman, Bobbie. I can write a book.

CT22.K25 2012   j809'.93592   C2012-901686-1

Library of Congress Cataloging-in-Publication Data

Kalman, Bobbie.
I can write a book about my life / Bobbie Kalman.
p. cm. -- (I can write a book series)
Includes index.
ISBN 978-0-7787-7993-3 (reinforced library binding : alk. paper) -- ISBN 978-0-
7787-8002-1 (pbk. : alk. paper) -- ISBN 978-1-4271-7884-8 (electronic pdf) -- ISBN
978-1-4271-7999-9 (electronic html)
1. Biography--Juvenile literature. 2. Authorship--Juvenile literature. 3. Books--
Juvenile literature. I. Title.

CT107.K35 2012
808.06'692--dc23

                    2012009586

Crabtree Publishing Company

www.crabtreebooks.com   1-800-387-7650   Printed in Canada/042012/KR20120316

**Published in Canada
Crabtree Publishing**
616 Welland Ave.
St. Catharines, Ontario
L2M 5V6

**Published in the United States
Crabtree Publishing**
PMB 59051
350 Fifth Avenue, 59th Floor
New York, New York 10118

**Published in the United Kingdom
Crabtree Publishing**
Maritime House
Basin Road North, Hove
BN41 1WR

**Published in Australia
Crabtree Publishing**
3 Charles Street
Coburg North
VIC 3058

Table of contents

A book about you

This book teaches you how to write a book about your life. You will enjoy writing this book more than any other because it is about you. Most books that tell a story are **fiction** books. Fiction books are made up from people's imagination. **Non-fiction** books give facts about many subjects such as history, animals, countries, cultures, and sports. Another kind of non-fiction book contains stories about real people. Your book will be this kind of non-fiction book. You may want to share your experiences with students at your school or write a book mainly for you and your family.

Your story will also include the story of your family.

Bobbie's story

I have been an **author** for many years, but long ago, I was a **refugee** and an **immigrant**. When I was nine years old, a **revolution** broke out in Hungary, the country where I was born. A revolution is a war against a country's government. My family and I had to escape in the middle of the night across the border into Austria, where we lived for several months. I wrote about my experiences in a **memoir** called *Refugee Child*. A memoir is a story about a special event or a period in a person's life, written from memories of personal experiences. A memoir is just one way to write a life story. What special event in your life would you like to share with others?

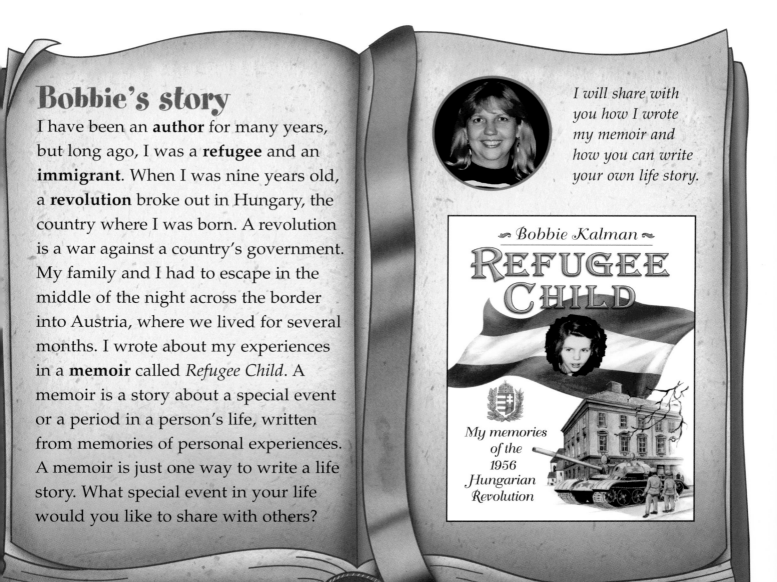

I will share with you how I wrote my memoir and how you can write your own life story.

~ Bobbie Kalman ~

REFUGEE CHILD

My memories of the 1956 Hungarian Revolution

Why write your story?

When you write a book about your life, it will not just be about you. It may include your family history, an important event, or a story that may help others. Writing a book is a great way to let others know who you are. Everyone has a story to tell. Some are exciting, and some will touch your heart. Some teach others about things they may not have known before. Besides being an author, you will also teach through your book.

Parts of a book

A non-fiction book has several parts and many pages. A book's pages are held together by a **cover**, or the outside of the book. When people see an interesting cover, they want to read the book. The cover below is the cover of this book. What pictures will you put on the cover of your book? What will be your book's title? A good title is clear, short, and interesting. Think about why others would want to read your book and write a title that will attract people to read it.

The back cover of the book may give you information about the author, **publisher**, price, and other books written by the author.

The **spine** of the book has the title, author, and publisher's name. It helps you find a book on a bookshelf.

The front cover of the book contains the title of the book and the name of the author. It catches your attention with an interesting title or a great picture or pictures.

The title page

The first page inside the cover is the **title page**. The picture on the right shows the title page of this book. What information does it give you?

Copyright page

The second page in this book is the **copyright** page. Copyright means that people cannot copy all or parts of the book without the author's or publisher's permission. What else does it tell you? Turn to the copyright page in this book and find the following information:

- the names of the people who helped create this book
- the addresses of the publisher
- the **dedication** of the book, or the words used to honor someone by placing his or her name in the book
- the **cataloging information**, a section of the page that tells the book's title, the name of the author, the year the book was published, and the type of book it is

Contents, glossary, index

The **table of contents** gives the names of the **chapters**, or sections, in the book and the page numbers on which they begin. The **glossary** is a small dictionary that explains special words used in the book. The **index** is an alphabetical list of the topics in the book with page numbers telling where those topics are covered.

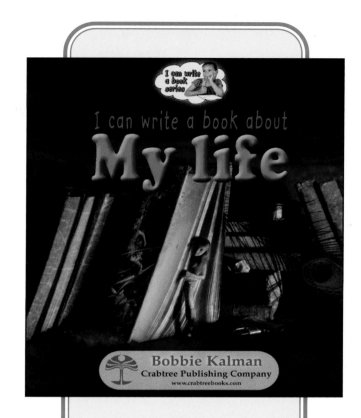

The page above shows the title page, and the page below shows the table of contents of this book.

Table of contents

Words to know

These two pages introduce you to some important words that you may need to use when you write your book. These words are usually found in a glossary at the end of a book. For your own book, you can do a picture dictionary with definitions underneath, like the examples on these pages, or a glossary without pictures, or both. (See pages 31 and 32 for more on glossaries.)

Ancestors are people in our families who were alive long before we were. We are their descendants, or family members who were born many years later.

A memoir is the written memory of events that took place during a special time in a person's life. The person who experienced the events is the author of the book.

An autobiography is the true story of a person's life. The book above is also a memoir.

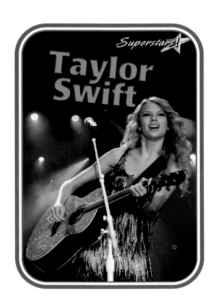

A biography is the true story of a person's life, written by another person.

A character is a person in a story. Culture is the way of life of a group of people.

Dialogue is the conversation that takes place between people in a story or play.

A **family tree** is a diagram that shows the relationship of family members such as children, parents, grandparents, and ancestors.

History is the story of events that took place in the past or a record of how people lived.

An **immigrant** is a person who leaves his or her native country and comes to another country to make a new life.

An **interview** is asking someone specific questions about his or her experiences or observations.

A **narrator** is the person telling a story out loud or in a book.

A **refugee** is someone who is forced to leave his or her country because of a war or other dangerous event.

The **setting** is when and where a story takes place.

Tradition is a set of beliefs or ways of celebrating that is passed down through families or cultures.

Different ways to write

To make your book more exciting to read, use the different writing styles shown on these pages. You can use one or all of them. No matter which styles you use, your book will have a beginning, middle, and an ending. The beginning introduces the subject or story and gives explanations. The middle part provides several chapters of information. The ending of your book may challenge readers with a message, an activity, or a look into the future.

Informational text

Informational text gives information. You could write your book mainly in this style and organize your ideas into small chapters called **spreads**. A spread is two pages that face each other. **Headings** tell the subject of the chapter. A **subheading** tells what a paragraph is about. The spread below is written in informational text. It is part of the introduction of my memoir. It gives information about my town and family, Hungary's flags and symbols, the language, and life under **Communist** rule. I also talk about the king, shown on the right, named King Kalman the Booklover.

King Kalman and I have two things in common. What are they?

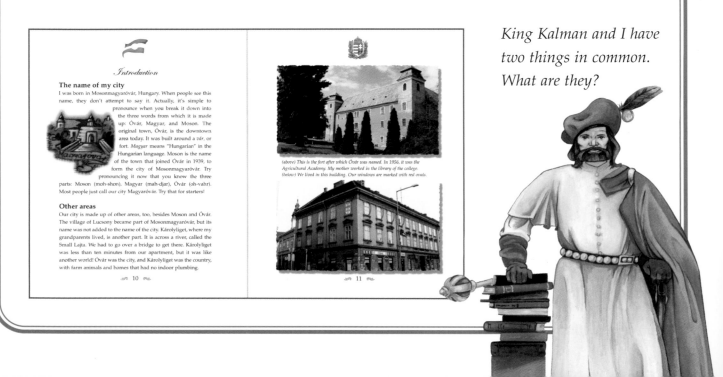

Introduction

The name of my city
I was born in Mosonmagyaróvár, Hungary. When people see this name, they don't attempt to say it. Actually, it's simple to pronounce when you break it down into the three words from which it is made up: Óvár, Magyar, and Moson. The original town, Óvár, is the downtown area today. It was built around a *vár*, or fort. *Magyar* means "Hungarian" in the Hungarian language. Moson is the name of the town that joined Óvár in 1939, to form the city of Mosonmagyaróvár. Try pronouncing it now that you know the three parts: Moson (moh-shon), Magyar (mah-djar), Óvár (oh-vahr). Most people just call our city Magyaróvár. Try that for starters!

Other areas
Our city is made up of other areas, too, besides Moson and Óvár. The village of Lucsony became part of Mosonmagyaróvár, but its name was not added to the name of the city. Károlyliget, where my grandparents lived, is another part. It is across a river, called the Small Lajta. We had to go over a bridge to get there. Károlyliget was less than ten minutes from our apartment, but it was like another world! Óvár was the city, and Károlyliget was the country, with farm animals and homes that had no indoor plumbing.

(above) This is the fort after which Óvár was named. In 1956, it was the Agricultural Academy. My mother worked in the library of the college. (below) We lived in this building. Our windows are marked with red ovals.

10

11

Narrative text

A **narrative** is a story. Autobiographies and memoirs are written mainly in narrative style. Narratives are filled with images that bring a story to life. They include setting, characters, dialogue, and a **plot**, or plots. A plot is the twists and turns in a story.

Story parts

The **body** of a narrative is made up of chapters that contain little stories, which are part of the big story. The first chapter catches your interest and makes you want to read further. It provides the setting and introduces you to some of the characters. The **climax** is the most exciting part of the story. The ending brings the story to a close with a message of hope, a surprise, or a glimpse into the future.

Descriptive text

Descriptive text describes a place or event using the senses of sight, smell, hearing, taste, and touch. The paragraphs on page 17 are written in descriptive text.

Instructional text

Instructional text gives directions on how to do something. The "notebook" on the next page contains instructional text about different type styles and handwritten words.

Writing poems

You may also want to include some poems in your book. I wrote *Refugee Child* as if I were a nine-year-old child, but I also wanted to share important ideas as an adult. I did this by introducing each chapter with a poem. The poems deal with important topics such as freedom, fear, secrets and lies, courage, choices, loss, truth, kindness, and love. The poem below is about **human rights**.

I never knew about human rights
or that I lived without most of them.
I never knew that it was my right
to live without fear or
discrimination *or force.*
I never knew about having the right
to own property or to get
an education of my choice or
about the right to leave my country.
I never knew about the right
to speak my mind or the right
to be proud of my culture.
I didn't know I had the right
to choose what I thought
was right for me.
I never knew
I had the right to be free.

Will you write or type?

If you are writing your book on a computer, there are many **fonts** from which to choose.

- A font is a style of type. Most of this book is written in a **plain text** font, but you will notice other kinds of fonts, as well.
- Words that are written in a **boldface**, or thick black, font are words that may be new to you. They are explained on the page or defined in the glossary at the end of the book.
- Headings and subheadings are in larger type. A different font is used to make them stand out from the rest of the text.
- **Fact boxes** give instructions, bring attention to special information, or ask questions. The fact boxes in this book are on notebook pages, like the one on the right.
- The text that gives information about a picture is called a **caption**. The captions in this book are written in *italics*. Words in italics slant to the right. The text below is a caption written in italics.

Will you write your book on a computer or by hand?

Fonts and writing

- If you are writing on a computer, try different fonts.
- Choose a plain text font that is easy to read.
- Choose heading fonts that suit your subject.

Chapter headings are in large colored type.

Subheadings are smaller than chapter headings and may also be in color.

- If you are writing your book by hand, use a thick pencil, pen, or marker to make words look like **boldface**.
- Write captions by *slanting* your words to look like an *italic* font.
- For headings, use markers or colored pencils.

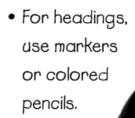

Images and memories

Most books are a combination of words and pictures. Before you start writing, look at some pictures in your family photo albums. Pictures can remind you of people or events in your life. They can also bring up certain emotions. These pictures reminded me of memories from my past. What memories might they trigger for you?

This girl reminds me of how I felt when I learned I had to leave my home, grandparents, and friends. Write a short story about a time you felt sad or afraid. What do you think this girl wrote in her diary?

My family loves to sing, and I love to dance. This man reminded me of my grandfather who often broke into song and wanted my cousins and me to be his choir. Do you have a relative who inspires your musical side?

Does your family sometimes act silly?

Write a story about how you and your family have fun.

What is an autobiography?

An autobiography is the true story of a person's life written by that person. When you write an autobiography, you are the author and main character in your book. Everyone has a story to tell, and your story matters!

Your voice matters

Your family and friends will want to read what matters to you and how you tell it in your own **voice**. Your voice is your attitude and point of view. It tells others that you have something important to say and are willing to express your ideas and emotions through your writing.

Where to start?

- Carry a notebook and write down any ideas that come to you.
- Make a list of the things you want to remember and the memories you want to share with others.
- If there is something important or dramatic that happened to you, you could write a memoir around that event. People will learn about your life and "hear" your voice through that event.
- Read about how I wrote my memoir on pages 16–19.

Little stories

Everyone has fascinating stories to tell! An autobiography is a life story that is made up of little stories.

- Make a list of the little stories in your life that you think others will enjoy. Record both happy stories and stories that made you feel sad.
- Start gathering the details of your stories by interviewing family and friends about their memories.
- Tell your stories in your voice. Don't be afraid to show emotion.
- Plan ways to make your stories fun by using art, activities, and photographs.

Think of little stories in your life that would help others deal with difficult situations or make them feel good.

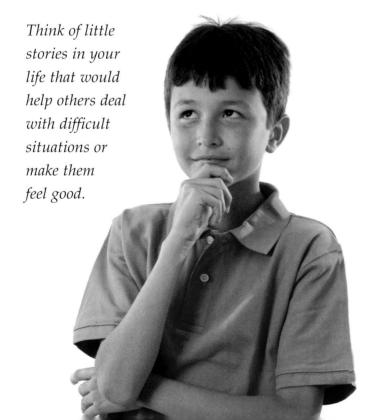

Inspiring stories

Many natural disasters take place each year, such as hurricanes, tornadoes, fires, floods, and earthquakes. In a disaster, people lose their homes, and some even lose family members. Disasters are sad and difficult, but they bring out the best in many people. People often gather together to help one another. The boy in the picture above was living in a **shelter** after a hurricane destroyed his home. He and some other young people volunteered to help serve food, look after small children, and clean the shelter. It made them feel good to help others. Do you have an inspiring story to tell? How have your acts of kindness made a difference to others? Use some of your stories to write your autobiography.

Writing my memoir

I was nine and my sister was seven when we became refugees. I am the child on the left.

In 1956, I had to leave my home, my town, my country, and many people I loved. I couldn't take much with me—only a few clothes and my doll. My family hid in the woods and walked over muddy fields for hours that freezing December night. We could hear machine guns and barking dogs all around us. Just before we reached the border, I had to throw away my bag with my doll in it and run for my life.

For years, I had nightmares about the night I escaped and lost my doll.

Why I wrote my story

Writing my memoir was a very important decision for me. Until I wrote *Refugee Child*, no other books had been written about the Hungarian Revolution in a child's voice. My nine-year-old voice wrote my memoir—not my adult voice. I knew it would be a very difficult book to write because, for many years, I had nightmares about that time in my life. My family and I did not talk about what happened to us, nor did most other families who became refugees. Writing my memoir made me face some of my fears and encouraged many other families to share their stories with their parents, children, and other relatives, as I did for the first time.

There was a full moon the night of our escape. We hid in the woods for hours from soldiers who were patrolling the border. The soldiers looked for refugees trying to cross from Hungary into Austria.

"Seeing" my story

I am a very visual person. I start every book I write by gathering pictures and visualizing how my books will look. When I started to write my memoir, I did not have a lot of pictures, but I had many **image details** filling my head. An image detail is a picture that sticks in your mind and grips your heart. Writing my memoir was a journey filled with fascinating images. I felt as if I was watching a movie in which I was the main character. I could visualize the settings, hear the dialogue between characters, and take part in the action.

*The first image detail I had of the Revolution was a parade that went past my school. My father was at the front of the parade. The flag he and other people were carrying had holes in the center. The symbol of the **Soviet Union** had been cut out to show that Hungarians wanted to be free from Soviet rule. Many people in the parade were killed that day.*

Soviet symbol cut out of flag

"Sensing" my story

Not only did I "see" visual images, I was able to remember the smells, tastes, sounds, as well as my feelings. For example, I started my story with a memory of a sunny October day. "My face felt warm, but I had a cold feeling in my heart." After school, I ran to the home of my grandparents, where my sister, grandmother, aunt, and I waited for our other family members to come home safely. We cooked dinner together and prayed everyone was still alive.

*The kitchen was filled with the most wonderful aromas! While the **goulash**, or stew, simmered, we helped Grandmama bake a plum cake. "How is it, I wondered, that we always feel loved in this kitchen?"*

17

Researching the story

Much of my story was written from my own memories, but I needed help with some details. I wrote my story in the **first person** and described everything that happened to me, but I also did a lot of **research**, or information gathering. On these pages are some of the ways I researched information for my memoir. You will need the help of your family and friends when you write your story. You may also have to read books, watch documentaries, and do Internet searches to find all the facts you need.

This was my school. An uncle who still lives in Hungary took this picture for me.

Family and friends

- I read my **draft**, or first copy, of each chapter to my mother to make sure my facts were correct. In some cases, we did not agree on details. I asked her many questions before I rewrote the chapters.
- I called aunts, uncles, and friends and asked them to share their memories of certain events at which I was not present.
- I asked family members to take photos of my town as it appears today. A friend who ran a tourist office was very helpful in sending me maps and pictures.
- I found the Austrian family who took us into their home during the Christmas holidays in 1956. They sent some pictures of us when we were in Vienna.

My mother reminded me about the Soviet tank that sat in front of our apartment building for several days. The tank let us know that the Soviets were back for good and that the Hungarian people had lost the Revolution. We left our country soon after that, knowing we could never be free under Soviet rule. More than 200,000 people left Hungary in 1956.

Learning about history

- I researched Hungarian history to understand more about my native country and why the Hungarian Revolution happened.
- I watched documentaries about the Hungarian Revolution, showing events that took place in Budapest, the capital city, as well as in Mosonmagyaróvár, the town where I lived.
- I researched how people crossed the border into Austria and the many ways that the Austrian people helped the Hungarian refugees.
- I searched the Internet for the ship on which I crossed the ocean on my way to North America. I even found menus from 1957, when I was on the ship.
- I watched video tours of the places I visited, such as Schönbrunn Palace, while I lived in Vienna as a refugee.

I am on the left. Beside me are other refugees from Hungary. Wonderful things happened to us in Austria! It was Christmas time, and I was given the greatest gifts—freedom, safety, kindness, and love.

I found a picture of the ship, the MS Berlin, on which I crossed the ocean.

Look for Bobbie's memoir

You can learn more about my memoir, listen to an audio visit with me, and read what other people said about *Refugee Child* at www.crabtreebooks.com. Just click on "About Bobbie Kalman" and you will find it all!

Start with an outline

Start writing your own book with an outline. Your outline will probably change many times, but it is a good way to collect your thoughts and know how you feel about them. List both your happy and unhappy "little stories." You could start with a simple outline like the one on the next page and change it to suit your own life. Make a list of questions to ask yourself to be sure you know what you want to write.

Food for thought

- Make a list of the things you want to remember and the memories you want to write about.
- Write down all the image details that pop into your head.
- Call or write people who may be able to help you remember details of your memories.
- Keep a diary of your life today so you can compare it with the past.
- Decide whether you want to write about your ancestors so you can better understand your life today.
- On a map or globe, find the country or countries of your ancestors and make your own map.
- Find out more about your culture.

In which countries has your family lived?

Sample outline

Who are the people in my family?

Who were my ancestors?

Where has my family lived?

What is my culture?

What are my favorite celebrations?

What do I like about school?

What are my favorite activities?

What makes me happy?

What important event in
 my life could I write about?

What are my hopes and dreams?

Why do I want to write my story?

How will my story help others?

Who are the people in your family?

What is your culture? Have you ever visited relatives in the country where your family once lived?

What kind of music do you like?

What kind of sports do you play?

Do you enjoy reading and writing? Are you writing a book about your life?

What makes you happy? Do you like helping animals? What are your dreams for the future?

Your family's story

You could write part of your family's story as a **documentary**, or factual report. Use some of the topics in the outline on page 21. Part of your book can be written in narrative style, part in informational style, and part in descriptive style. Comparing your life to that of your ancestors can also be interesting and fun. If you have a lot of pictures, you can do a **photo essay**. Photo essays tell stories in words that are placed under pictures.

great-grandparents

great-grandparents

grand-parents

Grandpa

Grandma

Grandma

Grandpa

Grandma

Dad

Paul

Carol

Mom

Liam

Me

Ask your parents to help you draw a family tree. Put the names of your family members in the circles.

Is your family big or small? Write about one of your family get-togethers in descriptive style.

Ask your grandparents if they have some interesting stories to tell. Did they like to play music together?

Compare your school to the school your great-grandparents attended. How are the schools the same? How are they different? What equipment did your great-grandparents not have at their school?

What fun things have you done with your family? Have you ever gone to a water park? Write about your experience in narrative style. Start with your trip to the park, talk about the different water slides, and tell why you enjoyed your time there. You could also tell stories about other theme parks you visited.

What is your culture? How do you celebrate it with your family and community? Write step-by-step instructions on how to celebrate a special holiday in your culture.

The youngest child in this family has special needs. He cannot walk or do many other things. His family loves him and looks after him. Is there someone in your family that needs your help? Write about how helping others helps you.

Stories past and present

A memoir is a lot like a movie. It creates visual images for the reader. Getting people "hooked" on your story or message is the first step!

The introduction

The introduction of your book should be exciting, mysterious, or informative to grab the attention of your readers. It gives the setting, or when and where the story takes place or starts out. Your main character, you, and some other characters in your story may be introduced through dialogue. Your introduction also **foreshadows**, or predicts future events.

Chapters with stories

Each chapter of your memoir tells little stories that are part of the plot, or the events in the main story. You may introduce more characters, move the story to other locations, or include new settings. Your little stories could include family events from the past that have become part of your life or events that changed your attitude or point of view.

Have you ever spent time at a pioneer village, living the life of your ancestors? How did you feel about doing laundry by hand and not having any modern machines to help you? Read some of Laura Ingalls Wilder's Little House on the Prairie books, then write a memoir of your pioneer experience using information you have learned from her memoirs. Compare your time as a pioneer to your life today.

If you are an immigrant, write a memoir about your life in your native country, how you came to your new home, and what traditions from your culture you practice today. Write about both happy and hard times.

*This family is celebrating Emancipation Day, the day slavery was **abolished**, or ended, many years ago. If your ancestors were slaves, do some research on what it was like to live under slavery. Write a family history comparing your life to the lives of your ancestors. Include the ways in which you celebrate this special day and how it makes you feel.*

Your research

- If you are writing a memoir about an event, research its history and make the history part of your story.
- Interview your family and friends for their memories of the event.
- Read a memoir such as the *Diary of a Young Girl*, by Anne Frank or *Refugee Child* to get a feeling of how memoirs are written.
- Watch videos about the event in your memoir to make sure your facts are correct.
- Search the Internet for information about the event you are writing about or a similar event.

*Is your family part of a native group? Do you take part in **powwows**? Write a story about the dances and other fun activities that you enjoy.*

If you were adopted, write a story about how you became part of your new family. Ask family members to help you write your story.

Share, revise, and edit

Once you have written your draft, it is time to read it to yourself. While reading, ask yourself these questions:

- Is my draft written in my voice?
- Have I used descriptive details so my readers can experience my story through their senses?
- Have I included my own observations and experiences, as well as those of my family?
- Do my captions describe what is happening in the pictures? Do they make my readers think?
- Did I use contrasts and comparisons?
- Did I write in various styles to make my story more interesting?
- Have I asked questions to make my readers think?
- How can I **revise**, or rewrite, my book to make it better?

Ask a parent or other family member to read your draft and help you with some details of your story. They can also help you organize and revise.

Read it out loud!

- After you have read your draft and made some changes, it is time to share it with others.
- Read your draft loudly and clearly at least twice.
- Ask your listeners to pretend they are on a treasure hunt. How many image details did they find in your story?
- Ask which parts of your writing were not clear.
- Ask your listeners to discuss your draft so they can give you suggestions on how to make your story better.
- How did the comments about your book help you?

Bobbie writes about emotions

If there are parts of your story that are hard to relive, leave them until you feel ready to write about them. You do not have to read these parts out loud to others if you do not want to. Writing a book is a journey filled with fascinating stories, but some of them may cause you to feel sad or anxious. After I wrote a few chapters of *Refugee Child*, I could not complete the most difficult one—the story of my escape. Instead of writing that chapter, I skipped ahead to write about the happy times I spent in Vienna. Writing my happy memories calmed me down and allowed me to go back and write the part of my book that was very difficult for me to relive.

*If you are not sure how to spell a word or whether you used the correct word, look it up in a dictionary. To find more interesting words for your book, use a **thesaurus**. A thesaurus gives **synonyms**, or words that have the same meaning as other words.*

Editing checklist

Editing is making sure your writing is clear and correct.

- Does your introduction make readers want to read more?
- Have you covered all the topics you intended to cover?
- Have you used interesting words?
- Do your sentences make sense?

Proofreading checklist

Proofreading is checking for errors such as spelling mistakes, capital letters, and **punctuation**.

- Are your sentences complete?
- Have you used the correct punctuation and capitals?
- Have you spelled names and other words correctly?

Designing pages and cover

Designing is making your book look good so people will want to read it. Using different fonts and colors makes the book attractive, but choosing good pictures to include is also very important. Pictures attract readers. Draw and paint your own pictures or take photographs of your home, family, and friends. Look at the design of this book to give you ideas about how to design your own book.

Download pictures

You can also download photos from the Internet. Ask a parent or teacher to help you find pictures that are free to use. Do a search of the kinds of art and photographs you need. When you download a picture, make sure you include the **source**, or where you found, the picture. Print the pictures and put them into your book.

Look through family photo albums and ask your parents or grandparents if you can use some of the photographs for your book. To make copies of old pictures, you can scan or photocopy them.

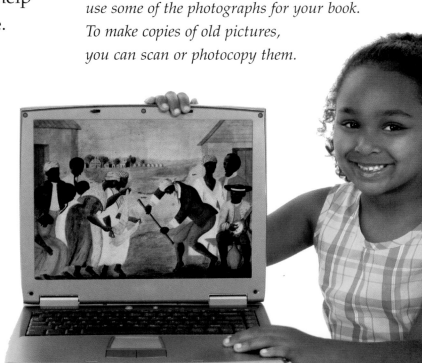

This girl researched her ancestors and wrote a book about her family history for Black History Month. She found this painting at commons.wikimedia.org/wiki/File: SlaveDance and_Music.

Cover and title page

You need to design a great cover and title page for your book. After you have completed these, ask your teacher or librarian to help you bind your book so others can read it. One easy way to protect your book is to place the pages in a folder with plastic page protectors. If you photocopy your pages before you slide them into the plastic sleeves, you will have your original copy from which you can make more books. Binders often have plastic pockets on the front and back, as well. You can slide your cover pictures into those. The spine will also have a thin plastic pocket for your title. On the right is a sample title page and binders. Below is a sample front and back cover with a spine.

title page

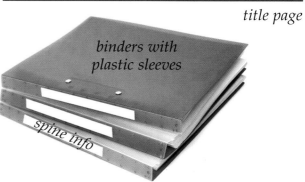

binders with plastic sleeves

spine info

About the author
Write something about yourself and why your book is special.

back cover

front cover

Publishing your book

Publishing your book is the last step. Many schools place the books students have written in the library for other students to read. Does your library have a publishing program for students? If you did your book on the computer, you could make an eBook that many students could enjoy.

Important pages

Before you publish your book on the computer or by hand, you will need to complete all the parts of a book. Look at the copyright page and table of contents at the front of this book. The glossary and index are on page 32. Page 31 gives you a review of how to do all these pages.

You may need to ask a parent or teacher to help you finish designing your book on the computer.

After you have finished your book, print off or photocopy all your pages. Use the photocopies for your book and save your handwritten pages and art. That way, you can make more copies if you need to.

Copyright page

Your copyright page will include all the people who helped you edit, proofread, and design your book: your family, friends, teacher, and librarian. This page may also include a dedication. To whom will you dedicate your book?

Table of contents

Your table of contents lists the headings of the chapters in your book. Their page numbers are placed at the right or left of the headings. Your table of contents is a revised list of your outline. (See the table of contents on page 3 of this book.)

Glossary

There is a picture dictionary on pages 8-9 in this book, but your glossary can just be words, like the glossary on page 32. Use a dictionary to define any new words that you did not know or your readers may not know. Sort your glossary in alphabetical order.

Index

The index is a list of the names and topics that readers may look for in a book. It is in alphabetical order and gives the page numbers of where the topics are. The index on page 32 will help you write yours.

Bobbie's reminder

The pages shown above are very important because they help your reader find and understand information in your book and thank the people who helped you. You can also include a **bibliography**, or list of books and their authors, that you used for your research. You need to include the sources of your photographs, as well. Use the information on the copyright page of this book to help you write your copyright page.

Glossary

Note: Some boldfaced words are defined where they appear in the book.

communist Describing a system of government that owns the property and goods in a country and denies its people many basic human rights, such as freedom of speech

discrimination The unjust treatment of people based on differences in beliefs, race, or culture

first person Words, such as I, me, or we, used by a writer or speaker to tell his or her own thoughts and experiences

powwow A native gathering celebrated with music and dancing

publisher A person or company that is responsible for printing and distributing a written book

punctuation The use of marks, such as periods or commas, to make the meaning of a sentence clear

shelter A building in which people who have lost their homes can stay until they are able to find a new home

Soviet Union A former communist country that included Russia and 14 other countries; also known as the USSR

Index